Little Bible Heroes™
Rahab

Written by Victoria Kovacs
Illustrated by David Ryley

B&H
KIDS
NASHVILLE, TENNESSEE

GOLDQUILL
WWW.GOLDQUILL.CO.UK

Published by B&H Publishing Group 2015. Text and illustrations copyright © 2014, GoldQuill, United Kingdom.
ghts reserved. Scripture quotations are taken from the Holman Christian Standard Bible ® Copyright © 1999, 2000, 2002, 2003,
2009 by Holman Bible Publishers. Used by permission. Printed in Heshan, Guangdong, China, December 2015
ISBN: 978-1-4336-8716-7   Dewey Decimal Classification: CE
Subject Heading: JOSHUA \ RAHAB \ BIBLE STORIES

Rahab lives in Jericho. Jericho is a big city with tall, strong walls. God tells the army of Israel to conquer the land where Jericho stands.

Two spies from Israel enter the city. They need a place to hide from Jericho's soldiers. Rahab bravely hides the spies on her roof.

Rahab tricks the soldiers by telling them the spies left the city.

Rahab then lowers the spies out the window so they can escape.

The spies tell Rahab to hang a scarlet cord from her window and gather all her family into her house. If she does, her family will be safe when Israel's army arrives.

When the army captures the city, the spies see the scarlet cord and know which house belongs to Rahab. She and her family are safe!

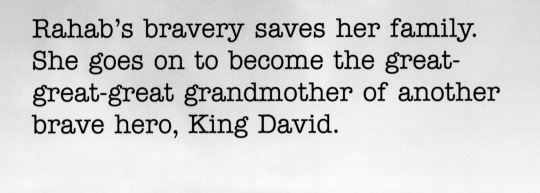

Rahab's bravery saves her family.
She goes on to become the great-
great-great grandmother of another
brave hero, King David.

Read:

Then she let them down by a rope through the window, since she lived in a house that was built into the wall of the city.
—Joshua 2:15

Think:

1. What do you think the city of Jericho was like?
2. Rahab is remembered for her good deed. Have you ever done a good deed?

Remember:

God wants us to help people, even when we must be brave to do so.

Read:

So the people shouted, and the trumpets sounded. When they heard the blast of the trumpet, the people gave a great shout, and the wall collapsed. The people advanced into the city, each man straight ahead, and they captured the city.—Joshua 6:20

Think:

1. How did Joshua obey God?
2. How do you obey God?

Remember:

God wants us to obey Him, no matter what.

Joshua was a great leader. He and his people obeyed God, and God gave them the Promised Land.

The walls of Jericho
fall down flat!

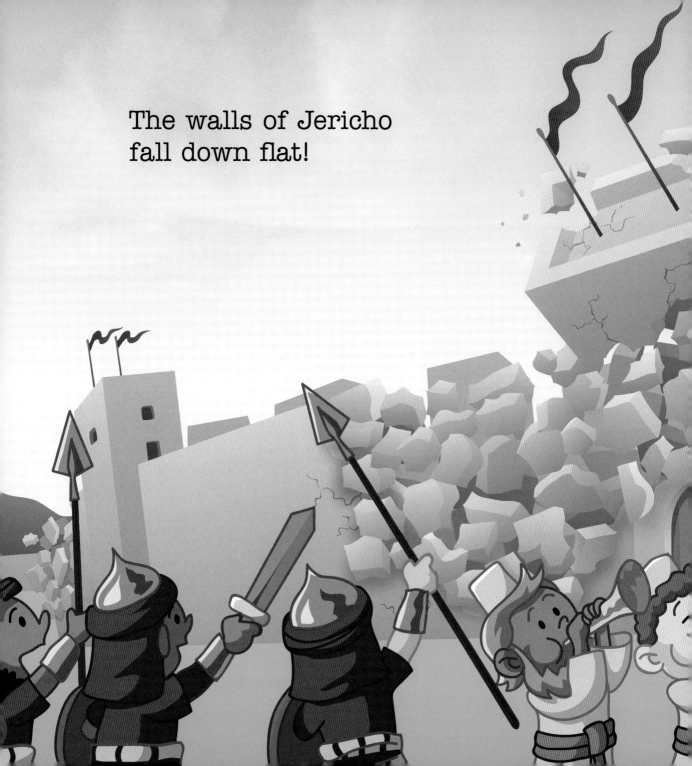

When the people reach Jericho, God tells them what to do. They obey. They march around the city for six days. On the seventh day, they march around the city seven times. The priests blow their horns. The people shout.

Joshua takes twelve stones from the river to make an altar. The altar is to remind the people how powerful God is and to obey Him.

The Israelites must cross the Jordan River to reach Jericho. When they carry the Ark of the Covenant into the river, God makes the river stop flowing! Everyone walks across on dry land.

Joshua sends two spies to explore the land and the great city of Jericho.

"Truly God has handed over all the land to us," the spies report. "The people of Jericho are terrified that we're coming."

God tells Joshua to lead the people of Israel into the Promised Land.

"Don't be afraid because I am with you," God says to Joshua.

Little Bible Heroes™
Joshua

Written by Victoria Kovacs
Illustrated by David Ryley

NASHVILLE, TENNESSEE

WWW.GOLDQUILL.CO.UK

Published by B&H Publishing Group 2015. Text and illustrations copyright © 2014, GoldQuill, United Kingdom.
ghts reserved. Scripture quotations are taken from the Holman Christian Standard Bible ® Copyright © 1999, 2000, 2002, 2003, 2009 by Holman Bible Publishers. Used by permission. Printed in Heshan, Guangdong, China, December 2015
ISBN: 978-1-4336-8716-7   Dewey Decimal Classification: CE
Subject Heading: JOSHUA \ RAHAB \ BIBLE STORIES